PROXY

PROXY

A Collection of Poems

Amrita Ganguly

Publications

KALPAZ PUBLICATIONS

Delhi - 110052

Proxy: A Collection of Poems

ISBN : 81-7835-502-7

Rs. 180

Published in 2006 in India by
Kalpaz Publications
C-30, Satyawati Nagar,
Delhi - 110052
e-mail : kalpaz@hotmail.com

Laser Typesetting at : Vinayak Printers, Delhi
Printed at : Salasar Imaging System, Delhi

Dedication

He rose from the ashes
And held in sway
The world
With his sheer brilliance
Mesmerised
I watched
And crafted words
Formed poetry
And watched on
As you danced
Every motion
A face of creation

Contents

PART-I: POEMS 2004

PART-II: THE JUNIPER TREE

PART-III: SCRATCH YOUR NOGGIN

PART-IV: A DIFFERENT PERSPECTIVE

PART-V: FOOTSTEPS IN SAND

PART-VI: MOTHBALLS AND MISTRESSES

PART-VII: I AND U TRUE BLUE

PART-VIII: WORLDS

PART - I

POEMS 2004

1
Celluloid Dreams

The big screen flickers
may everyone have a wet dream
the camera pans
looking beyond the star, into him
how many casting couches
how many to claim
in his call to fame
that he was a great piece of ass
full of strut and sass
sweet-talking mama
who gave head good
great at making a fire
without using wood
he performs to please
drawl put to perfection
one day he knows
he'll have real attention

and they'll all cream
just looking at him
these are his celluloid dreams
the path to the top is rough
it sees many a downy bed
and many a rough sack
you wanna stroll down the Walk of Fame
and listen to blues on the Boulevard
ah! Hollywood!
everyman's broad
yours to climb
yours to mount
till you reach the top
you got talent
you got what it takes
you're in Hollywood
but you gotta make your own breaks
pimping peddling on the side
your agents your best buy
a line of coke to see you through the day
that $100 gotta see you a long way
but you aint quitting
cause you're celluloid dreaming

you work the agents
try the studios
play bit lines
wash dishes
you want success
you want all that you see
and you got what it takes–all grit and sweat
on screen and off.
you know you're your best bet
so keep celluloid dreaming
and keep winning!

2

The Shadow

The light is fading

i am silhouetted in the moonlight

while others love

and they see me poised against the ball of green cheese

sliding down the slopes of wantonness

and i enter their private fancies

what is he thinking?

she?

the fledglings withering apart

torn

by the shadow of a silent tugging desire

3
Speaking without Words

When did the words die out?

when the walls came up

and the onslaught of heavily armourred soldiers

could no longer overcome their great heights

and swords and helmets clanking

they fell

on their own once again

some silently gloating in their solitariness

others quietly yearing for solidarity

but each unable to overcome the

hostile barrier of the self

4

Metroraiders

We fight for a place
urchins under our designer clothes
what are our fears?
that we will be displaced?
that we will be subjugated?
that we will have nowhere to go?
and noone to care?
so we keep the world at bay
a shroud of materialism.
of procuring, hording, storing
to cover the terror
and Simon and Garfunkel
belt out the sound of silence.

5

To All the Beautiful Ones

Not everything has to be planned with the long
term view

live each joyous moment to the hilt, for what it is

for none knows what the morrow brings.

One second mere humdrum earthling

The next, heavenly nymph.

6
A Man's Life

Man prances away from his shadow
but it follows
he stumbles away drunkenly from his thoughts
but they weave after him, running
he tries to dodge himself
but his image is caught in the mind
there is no escape
from his innards
man may rebel
but he merely conforms to years of revolt
man might be a monk, locked up in a monastery
but he's merely fighting the undercurrents
of mundane life
a man may be a preacher
so? what of it?
at Confession
his thoughts wander to his own mortality
what is man?
well?

7
The Final State

I look at the gnarled, wizened faces
of the miniscule gnomes
who inhabit the corners of my room
in their curled elfin shoes
with their gigantic deformed genitalia
dancing in a Druidical circle
around a cauldron bubbling under a toadstool –
and they whisper to me as they canter
in Elysian Murmur:
"after such knowledge, what forgiveness."
the world is an extension of myself
the merry-go-round
goes round and round and round
and up and down and up. down
the stallion bobs prettily, subdued into gaiety
a gaiety charged with man-made electricity
and the leopard gently wags its tail with a content
sigh

and i'd like to get of whirling piece of ostentation
just get me off this crap shoot
but i am locked
or am i?
do we lock ourselves?
they say your first love never dies
but flames abounded and the wolf howled blood
thirstily to the
full moon
sinister happenings at midnight
the tap of the door
all i wanted was to be loved
and i heard his voice in the wilderness
"i love you"
if only twere true
now i walk
one step, two steps, three steps
down the middle of the dusty lane
footprints to be eradicated in the next desert
storm
i to disappear
and perhaps in the next thousand years
i shall attain nirvana
the final state

8
Today's Tower

Wallflowers

plastered to the wall

no say

drunks plastered

lolling on the ground

nowhere bound

home? where? what?

plastered limbs

held together with silt and sand

this is where the war ended

this is where the war began

we speak the same tongue

but not the same language

we listen

but do not hear

we look

but do not see

'look, look, look at that amputated man

look, look, look at vice, crime and sin

gangrene sets in on the limb

and the amputated man

is swallowed up within the fissures of the waste-
land

but all man said was

"let doves cry, cry, cry

what a good life."

He looks beyond his wife to the mistress

she looks beyond the kids

to the hidden farthing

children kill flies for sport

and the Gods jest at man's inquest

and all man says

is

"let doves cry.'

(Do you hear them?)

9
Look and You Shall Find?

Life goes on

people move on

the genii of appearances

victors over the genii of truth

but truth is

appearances disintegrate

in the niggling centre of the mind

alone in a lonely, lamplit night

straight down a crooked path I walk

into a rosebush of thorns

10
Infidelity Again

I look at the blank page
and words squeeze out
painfully
from my pen
i'm thinking back on memories
and slowly they'll take form, shape, realness
the day i took the man of another woman
you who do not know who i am
and hopefully never
you,
part of the womanhood
you,
my companion in the first blood and last betrayal
such are the vagaries of life
you,
who do not know of me
and I,
who have caught you
but fleetingly

11
A Woman's Song

We danced all night
my man's so fine
but when dawn came
my sugah man was gone
gone the sweet loving
gone–
he's out hustling
gone to a wife and three kids
gone to comfortable digs
and i reach out to the lonely side of my bed
waiting for the next time he leaves town on
    'business'
I need a drink
Jack Daniels is a pal of mine
who keeps me company when noone comes by
go to the office
my boss is black and hard

buy hey is saying black and hard
equal to discrimination?
will i be charged in front of the whole nation on
television?
why, i don't see!
black is beautiful to be
and a man gotta be hard to be good
so why the doo-dee sing song
I'm just a lone lady in town
in this world
has empowerment
come around yet?
walk into the bar
some like cooking
others like hooking
can't take this lonesome shit no more
and then he walks in
I light a cigarette
and take a slug of my drink
much later, my strapless dress lies in a pile on
his floor
did he pick me up
or did I him?
empowerment?

does it exist?

i see you beautiful people frown

you who live of the rich side of town

well made up like a well laid table

and the napkin

on the lap

with the hopes

to disguise the farting

well i get hitched to him

tired of solitary nights

two's company

but what about that third man

creeping around in my mind

some learn to make it

I learn to fake it

is security really a substitute for some wild screwing?

and the man in mind

plays his tin drum

banging crashing beating

i tell my kid:

"never trust a man who can't take you home.

never trust a man who takes you home to soon".

The daughter graduates summa cum laude

and moves out of home. takes up that plum job

the boy marries his girl –

you find her just a churl

your man you have to drive to work and back

and make his tea sharp at half past

what you got woman

well

you got

no job (emancipation hasn't come around after all.

he's got his pride as the family earner

and relegated to you be the bread burner)

no joy

no Jack (can't let he kids on that you were a lush around town)

you got just the vibrator (cause he'd rather read the papers)

so you just have the best satisfaction money can buy

made in Japan

what you really have, woman?

you got noone by your side.

12

Voices (In Memory of Mimi)

Lost voices, wordless
the aftermath
of raised voices
fading into the background of irrelevance
after the war
silence
picking up the threads from where we left off
or trying to, struggling
a farce, lost and blurry within ourselves –
things will never be the same again

13
Mr. Moon

Mr. Moon
When you look at me
tell me
what you do see
do you see a whore
in New Orleans?
do you see
the First Lady
at tea?
do you see
a native
of Afrique?
or
do you see
the trappings
of a queen?

do you see in me
every woman
when you look at me?
do you see my heart breaking
as the waif on the street
clings to me
for a farthing?
in every lifetime
i have been one of them
and they of me
do you see, Mr. Moon?
do you see?
when I dream
come with me
take each of me
to your shores
and set us free

14
I, The Fool

They pick me up

they put me down

respectively

when i'm

in

and

out

but

i

remain

constant

for

i

am

the

fool

jesting myself and others into a smile

happiness

only a frame of mind

yearnings fulfilled in the speck of an eye

the truth settled in diplomatic guise

but i

remain

constant

forever true to myself

knowing that tomorrow once again

the sun will rise and set

the stars shall shine

but man

will be forever man

delusionary

always in search of a laugh or two

and that's where i come in

i, the fool

15
I'm No Saint, My God Sleeps

I'm no saint, my god sleeps
yet i try, mere mortal.
i will not speak
words of anger to you
words of haste
but thoughts bubble around
in the seething cauldron of my mind
teeming with fury
like a toad
which traps a fly with a long sticky tongue
to be purged
but a residue of the mutilation remains
after all, i ain't no saint
looming, my private Devil, time and again
i want to forget the rage inside
dont gimme no more pain

16
The Long and Short of It

Delusion shatters into reality;

but reality, a mere illusion

what is the truth then?

is peace just an opiate of pain?

is life just a seed of the universe?

is love just the beginning of the end?

what is the truth?

what is true?

17
Life

He was toiling hours in the scorching sun
breaking stones, spreading tar
muttering to himself:
"you she-dog broad
you give me a fire in my loins–and release is
hard come by
you give me the skies–
and the moon winks at me every nightfall
you give me faith–
to be shaken by storms
i reach out to touch you, to grasp you to my heart
but coquette, you are an illusion."
and the rythm of the chaingang spoke, clanking
chains and machines in sync:
"you are born
with the right to live, a free man
the right to dream

and hope
the right to build
yet you bind yourself
in your quest for money, power, supremacy
you fight battles and street wars
you destroy, desecrate
this then is your fate,
living bound to the chains you place around your
own ankles
you are your own master; you are your own
slave".

18
The Wench (1)

Do you see the woman standing

in the doorway

at half past midnight

the moon throws a shadow of yellow, iridiscent light

yawning upon her

as though in boredom,

saying: "these things do happen, righto!"

he alights from his carriage

in ten minutes time

the London fog swirling

in the silent night

and the watchman checks the street lamps

and that all's well with the world

the wench

dressed in plain black

a mascot

to the house of fallen girls

a place in time and reality
and every cad's memory
a few pennies clattering
as the footsteps die away

19

The Wench (2)

Who is the fallen girl?

one who sells her body?

or one who sells her soul?

one who peddles ass?

or one who allures with vice?

one who raises her flesh and blood

by her flesh and blood

flesh

blood

or

the high class dame

who destroys the foetus in her womb,

thinking it to be a hindrance to her queenly ways?

20
My Dream

I hear myself in the depths of the silent night
when not even dogs bark
i who have spent a thousand nights in purgatory
drunk wine in Venetian cafes
as the gondolier
sings by the wharfside
in the final reckoning it it your deeds
merged in the momentum of thronging millions
which free you from the common slop of mediocr
ity
if i give to greed and vice
in every streetcorner i have an addiction
if i give to penance
i free myself from desire
if you have hope
build your dream
and if you're going by the rope

go like a man
what good now worldly possessions?
there's a good market for dusters and dustcloths
in the world.

21
Innocence

There were the parties in Austria
and skiing on snow-clad slopes
warm, spiced cider
intoxicating the evenings by the fireplace
and before you know it
a cousin becomes a lover
we make small talk, the morn after
avoiding the eye
an inflamed, secret stupor for the night,
for forbidden yearnings of wordless desire
memories to hang heavy and silent
nary a word to be spoken
lest the perfect innocence
of this reality
be lost

22
Infidelity

What infidelities
lurking
in the dark lamp-lit street corners
of the imagination?
planes of existence
clandestine meetings in crowded street cafes
too much wine
and you're retching your guts out
she no longer sleeps with you
the other man,
yet come by,
a phantom lover.
between the desire
and
the reality
falls the betrayal.
the closing in

of two strangers
silhouetted
in the falling light
in a celebration
of
liberation
life

PART-II

THE JUNIPER TREE

23
Occupational Hazards

"OK, up against the wall, fellah"
the prison warden
barks at the convict
"Lethal weapon concealed on the body"
she singsongs out loud
her hand on his fly
... scoring a high
on private property?
she just wants to get lost with the key
Beware!
As a doctorate of philosophy
I have made an intense study
on the voyeuristic impulse
of the homo sapien,
or man,
as he is otherwise known
to begin with –
a slide show

watch the three in a tub
rubadubdub
watch the insatiable amazonian
get into his thong
tied and chained
he is in sheer ecstasy
even as his wife passes by
this double bondage sure is his high
well what are the dangers
of his pleasure
you ask yourself in reflection
I pose this question to you;
"has any one ever died from dehydration
from losing too much spunk?"
perhaps it would have been better
had he been a monk;
To come to Lotty,
a mother of two
of course everyone knows
of the vibrator
but Lotty?
she prefers a vacuum cleaner
can you beat that!

not to clean out the cobwebs of course
hubby sill gives her a weekly score
but her vacuum cleaner
as he's known to the mob down town
well, he's slick, fast and smooth
and has her coming and drooling all over him
in a sustained swoon
why! he's even better than a Japanese machine
but the risks of his exercise are great
if hubby finds out
he'll be eating dirt
as good as dead;
the astronaut
leaving gravity behind
prances around nude on the moon
with only his oxygen nozzle
in place
the other,
gravity having been left behind,
standing to attention like a soldier,
defying the Newtonian mind,
though it would be a pity indeed
if he were to be read wrong

and be buggered by Martians from outer space
putting an end to his endangered race
The computer whiz kid
pushes those buttons right
skillfully plays games,
rams
drives in the hard disk
experiments with software
and soon before know it, you're THERE;

24
Equal Opportunities 1

They left for foreign lands
the lands of honey and plenty
he became a cabbie
insultingly called 'paki'
and they make out on his back seat
full of hot blood and heat…
but he has to pay the bills
and espouses middling philosophy
in order to appear yuppie
but his sons
ah! his sons
to whom the golden rules of immigration
he has imparted
they look to the old land
and profess the old religion
and look for traditional girls as brides
in the land from which they have departed

the white chicks are OK by them–
but only to play a game
they love beef in their burgers
as long as its kept out of the house
and one nighters are fine
but they'll never give up
their legally wedded wives.
but when Dad proposes a merger
for his doting daughter
and the tycoon's son
she rebels, leaves home
and cohabitates with a 'bum'
in their terms
... so much, for equal opportunity

25

Equal Opportunities 2

Away from the ghettos, the progm, the torture

they fled

the glinting Statue of Liberty ahead

he put up his butcher shop

at the corner of the deli

good kosher food like they used to have back home

she gave painting lessons

to the fading genteelity

and together they lived

with memory of the old country

between them

they had courage, love, strength

to start all over again

you gotta live for yesterday, today and tomorrow.

If you wanna up in life

and not spend sleepless night

worrying about life's if's but's –

learn from the past!
well Maria and Johann
were gifted with two sons
and the two sons
grew up
right in Hell's Kitchen
birth leads to the issue of survival
and only the strong survive
Wilhelm
was the biggest boy in school
he topped class
broke glass
but got along with both teachers and students
without fuss.
Paul
he was a painter and dreamer
and had to be rapped
for not doing his work
he suffered from cold
and a weak constitution
and sought older brother's protection
after Wilhelm
graduated from school and went away
little Paul.

had no one with whom to play
he went to work part time at his father's shop
(now expanded by hard work)
and spent the rest of his time,
painting on New York Wharf
soon the cousin Humboldt
came into the scene and
chose Wilhelm
to inherit part of her father's
ammunition factory –
it had seen huge profits in the war
Fraulein Humboldt was the toast of town
but would have sacrificed anything to have Wilhelm
go down
News of this soon reached the old folks
who still simple at heart
wondered how they could face their neighbours
who had promised Wilhelm their daughter
Paul was not to be out done –
he befriended lady Wilbury
of Englandshire
and so together the two got bethrothed
but not all was fine

Paul discovered that his charcoal and paints
suited him better
for the wick
on his paintbrush
was the only wick
he could dip
so much for equal opportunity!

26
Clown Town

The circus has finally come to town
It's totally clown town now
see those two midgets
diminished in size
since I last met them 10 years ago
they converse in stifled statements,
for I am the only
not embroiled in matrimony
nor incarcerated in an nunnery
or in the practice of celibacy
"shocking! shocking!" I hear them say
i take a sip of my drink
and look around
There's Toony,
playing the fool
his wife in a mink jacket
so much for preservation –
she's also very well preserved

People enquire politely about my employ
I tell them I work for a goy
they ask about my mode of transport
I tell them I've come by oxencart
but then,
I have the last laugh
"And I think you've got some of the dung
on your shoe" I state,
"No? oh dear,
I hope that it isn't you,"
I do not have a swimming pool in my place
I do not drive a fancy car
I do not dine at Maxims's thrice a week,
I'm just an ordinary hick,
and happy to be on my own
cause I get the best laugh out
of these guys
and the married man coming on there can go
sleep with his wife.

PART-III

SCRATCH YOUR NOGGIN

27
Moving Forward

Samba woman

Moving to the rhythm

Black lovah man

Working the chaingang

Chocolate coloured children

Playing in the park

It's a long way from being a darkie

To whitey turf

But like they say

'We're gonna do it, mama.'

28
The 12 Faces of Time

(1)

A flash from a meteor

and in the beginning there was a second

tick-tock, tick-tock

and then another

and a third and a fourth

and a day rolled by

and God created

swampy underbushes and marshes

dinosaurs walking the breadth of the land

"Let there be light",

And there was light

"Let there be music,"

And there was music

"Let there be man,"

And that is where the fun began.

(2)

the Garden of Eden is now as bare

as the rears of Adam and Eve before the fall.
In the beginning there was a tadpole,
losing itself in its moist pond.
If in advertising, conception differs from expecta
tion,
you're a goner
the same for child birth
tick-tock, tick-tock
and a newborn babe becomes either a child
prodigy
or just a number on someone's social security
card
and with time you become a surrogate parent.

(3)

the Child Krishna
dancing around his gopis
meandering flute —
stealing buttermilk
the needs of survival are very strong
the unprejudiced eyes of children,
but then tick-tock,
reality, catches up
and the curtain drops.

(4)

he doesn't understand why his father whips mama

and doubly more, why she doesn't protest.

In school, they call him dragon head

cause he's always seething within.

he can't understand why the cop at the corner

keeps a strict

vigilance on him

he certainly can't see the knife in his pocket.

"Dago s.c.b." someone cusses.

he gets up slowly, but is stopped by the gaze of the copper.

Tick-tock, tick-tock, the clock never stops

(5)

In his Sophomore year

he falls in love

she doesn't know he exists

he heads for the cheap side of town

for $ 20.00 he can dip his wick in another pot of wax.

Tick-tock.

(6)

Wall street collapses

no more white collar banking jobs

he joins the family business

no self-respecting Catholic girl gives him a
  second glance

despite his brand new Mustang

and high class ways.

(7)

He finally marries someone outside the
  community

a nice Jewish girl,

whose father the Rabbi promptly disowns them

he eats kosher meat

and makes out on the kitchen table

as well as with the waitresses in his nightclub

he goes for red-haired dames

it's the only way to find out whether the colour's
for real

or out of a bottle.

(8)

In the beginning

God created an atom

which grew into Hiroshima

In the beginning, God created an atom

which grew into man.

Putrefaction has set in

he can't even crap on his own.

(9)

The epitheth on his tombstone:
"May his soul rest in peace."
But he was one ornery man
where will he go?
Up? down? this man about town?
It is the age of Kalyug.

(10)

There was a lizard born,
during the marigold, sunshine days.
It creeps around, blinking
once the seeker, now the sought.

(11)

The tombstone is slayed down
by storming nocturnal lightning
down the tomes of history
an infant was rushed to survival
on a sleet pelted night
protected by a serpent.

(12)

What is reality?
the shrink points to his Buddha:
"May the cycles of the soul set you free"
the lizard dies
and an ant is born.

"May the cycles of the soul set you free"

the lizard dies

and an ant is born.

29
Forever

"Oh master, sell me a dream," I cried to the merchant.

The merchant raised his plumed head

Amidst his treasures

and said kindly

"Alas, my friend, dreams are not mine to sell

For they cost nothing and yet are priceless.

They will drive you to plough your fields harder

even in the hot midday sun.

They will make man walk with his head held high

For there is hope in his soul.

They will be the plinth of your life

My friend, spend your gold on pettier things...

for dreams cost nothing but are priceless

and are not mine to give."

30
The Wall

Limitations exist only within the mind:

They are your greatest handicap, unconquered;

defeated, they open up a whole new world to you.

Never just sit there

watching the wheels go turning by.

PART-IV

A DIFFERENT PERSPECTIVE

31
A Battered Woman

Woman

Flesh of man

She gets up to her alarm clock

Has to take the dog for a walk (even on a cold wintry morn)

Reads the papers over her morning coffee

Kisses the two-timing slime off to office.

Rushes the kids to school

Rushes off to work (they could do with the extra dough)

Rushes back home to fix dinner

Which she waits for him

He ain't coming back to soon

Too busy humping his boss

And after all this

She can be granted a mere affair

With the man next to her in the carwash

In keeping with expectations of daily routine

He comes back late

Pissed

Frustrated his affair ain't going the way it should

She tries to understand

But he wallops her across the face

Tears off her clothes and roughly screws her

And falls into a deep snore.

A battered woman

Our rights?

32
Destination Unbound

Drunk again
A mad stampede of faceless strangers
I squeeze into the train among them
Tearing up my privilege pass
What a relief
To smell hard-work perspiration
To feel the grime
To touch common ground again
Sights like memories whizzing past
I take off my Gucci scarf
And give it to the amputated girl on crutches
A smile
It's been so long since someone smiled
I do not know my destination
Only that I want to go where 'this is not here'
I take the last swig of my whisky
"A little country liquor?" the hobo in tattered overcoat next to me.

I do not want to know where I'm going.

Only to where "this is not here."

PART-V

FOOTSTEPS IN THE SAND

33
Dimensions

In that tormented twisted coldly feverish Scottish Castle
alienated proudly atop mossy boulders
on the highlands
where each chilly gust has a tale to tell
to the locals, who bending for firewood,
avert eyes from the Scottish Castle,
tiptoe silently the ghost of yore
by the damp fireplace
where a roast of years ago
adorns the spit
the table seat with the finest of linen and silver
for the guest who never arrived
Today,
I sit in my lamp – lit den.
The bricks come alive with a resume of my life
bulging out in spasmodic renditions
of various stories

The room is as you left it

There's only been a little heartbreak added to it

The times you didn't turn up, or so I thought

Like the guests who never arrived

But you were there a long time ago

And I was too blind to see it.

34

Sundown in Nevada

The cool setting orange breeze rifles my hair in the silence

Soothing searing, tormented passions

as I sit in front of my easel

tumbler of whisky placed conveniently nearby

my short dressing gown raised above the thigh

full boobs partway hanging out

my legs parted around the corner of my perch

on the porch of my hacienda

purple - capped mountains looming in the dis

tance

brush in hand

mind in recess

as I paint a stroke and then another

earth colour, my colour

an orgasmic calm

I'm a hack artist in a hack world

will they ever look to see?

Well, my friend, this is Nevada

This is life

This is the gamble —

You'll never know until you try.

35
MCP

The first round and then the second
Until the world feels like a merry-go-round
You forget the paparazzi
Until oops ! You have to make that fast getaway
Won't do to be all over the morning papers
With the starlet on your arm
While your wife… well, you stop to think:
"When was it really that the passion went out?"
You weave and totter in your drunken, dazed state
"God, she's young enough to be my daughter!"
The monkeys pop the peanuts into their mouths
The camels store up the water —
the piglets are gonna oink their way to that shrink
in Beverly Hills tomorrow
And you, the middle aged swine, tell the disappointed girl
that you need all the energy stored up in your schlong

to work better

and send her packing off in a cab.

36
Silence 2

She watches him on the deck chair next to her.

Through her dark glasses.

Pink gin in hand

On their private beach on the Riviera.

Brown hair finely matted on his chest

Tapering hips.

Long muscled legs.

His black bulging swimming briefs.

Hmm...

Her thoughts run asunder.

He watches he silently unobserved.

through the drapes of their mansion

He can read her mind.

His wife.

The silence.

They meet for lunch.

Aimless chatter, small talk

he, forever the gracious host, the attentive husband.

"Will it be today?" he idly wonders.

Perhaps,

they will slip away to a private hideout

she, on the pretext of shopping

he, on the plea of urgent business.

the silence

he retires to his room

this zig - zag

Where does it begin and end?

Is it the deed or the thought itself?

37
The Flipside

Lily white lilacs sprout out amidst the dung and
decay
the fairy-winged water-baby flocks asleep
in the drain water
nuptial bells ring ding-dong ding-dong
the precedence of another chiselled gallows
the cow jumped over the moon —
thus green cheese and holy shit
Step in to the sacred waters for a cleansing dip
And all you'll be blessed with is only crap
galore in your hair.
the pearl in the oyster is clammed from the world.
the black buck runs pursued.
And you suffer a massive coronary going
though the mind staggering bills.

PART-VI

MOTHBALLS AND MISTRESSES

38
PMS

I hitched a ride to the moon
because I couldn't find a phone
and decided to go via satellite
to cuss you and your very clan —
charge me for defamation if you can.
I climbed the highest mountain
to get a birds-eye view
and dived to the depths
of the deepest ocean
to get a sharky - sharky, thingy - thingy, thongy - thongy
thing going with you
you gave me
jetlag
vertigo
and cramps
and I ritually
claw out your honey brown eyes
every month, the year round.

39

Mothballs and Mistresses

(1)

there exists in a dacha
in Stroika
a metallic robot
made by man
in the form of man
jumpstarted by his third leg
he sustains on
black bread and vodka neat
and secretes liquid rust
in his aged daily ministrations
as woman, created in the form of woman
will not give this wheezing clunking block
a second glance,
he, being guided by his third leg
and she, by her third eye.

(2)

In the Jongian era

it is difficult to discriminate

between man-made in God's eye

and woman, in man's eyes.

At 15:

If only the French would remain French

and not 'phile' themselves with such ease:

I'll me demande: 'Permettez – moi ...'

Well, I gotta say, if you have the technique you're on the make

But this imitation, I feel, knew only how to shake.

(3)

Swinging like a pendulum

in equal degree

although the preacher raises brimstone and fire

against infidelity.

(4)

the doublecrossers

men

they'd give anything for a.b.j.

and if you don't

there are always sandwiches and cocktails

minorities expanding –

if you're upper crust

stay away.

(5)

to come now to married man

or to be more precise.

you,

well I hope you're ready for this-

the sudden phone call out of the blue

meeting the real mama in the park

I think I'll ask her to change your unthongy - thongy multi-coloured jocks

why be a closet joker?

I'm laughing from here to Timbuctoo

where you last poked - her.

(6)

middleaged men are the worst

their womenfolk being menopausal

they reveal their drunken lust

to the young and nubile

and just a small warning to the ladies in question

don't comply! For the bank balance, properties and high life

will all go to the wives

and for the really gutsy -

he'll die in the middle of a lawsuit

from cardiac arrest

and leave you worth even more the less.

(7)

my torn, mangled, ripped moorings

screeching

I appeal to you –

the beast in man

to set me free.

40
Upon Matrimony

The businessman says for profit or loss
The engineer says have to put the nuts into the
bolts
The geologist goes down under—the great
Barrier Reef and all
the train conductor goes full steam ahead
the musician loves to fiddle around
the playboy-well, all that gel has to be for some
thing
the playgirl-loves a mustang
the lawyer specialises in divorce cases –
who knows how much alimony (read also pali-
mony)
todays feminist writer loves a pen
the doctor gets ready with the fertility injection
and you would rather swear by the *Kamasutra*
than subject yourself to convention.

PART-VII

I AND YOU TRUE BLUE

41
The Playing Grounds

I pass through the rooms of my memory

fleeting around in the broken down, dilapidated villa

ah! the war, it was bad.

i bury the dead

with my tales of majestic ruins

saving what exists

what is fact? what is reality?

what is truth? what is perspective?

the moonbeams reflect

limbless statues

peeping in through the gaps in the ceiling

as i chronicle voices from the past:

"he'll take good care of you now".

my lover, leaving me with a knowing smirk, to his

best friend.

"you play off one group against the other".

my mother's brother, the copper, throwing me
down fifth floor
stairs.
"I know the art..."
the perverted, tongue-wagging, foul-breathed,
moonfaced shrink i abhor.
"If only i were a bachelor..."
The married man i had an affair with
giving me the kiss-off, the deed complete.
"I fell'.
At school, two days after being beaten black and
blue.
"they gave me shocks cause they found me
smoking a
cigarette" –
the junkie at the asylum. i doubt she still lives to
tell her tale.
'whore!"
after being raped.
do you hear the echoes?
empty the womb
empty the soul
empty the heart
empty the mind.

42
Song of Wrath

Screw the system
I am the furious, destructive wind
screeching like a banshee
fanning flames till man burns himself out
none shall have power over me.
usurped or otherwise
no man
who
beats and fornicates
beats and fornicates
beats and fornicates
both wife
and sister
alike
i break bonds which bind
I snap telephone connections
of whispered relays
of

information
i hack into your secret domain
there is no peace for you
there is no redemption
uproot you and sweep you away
in my wrath
i shall
toss you
like debris
upon
the garbage heaps
that litter the years of my life
and let the sewer rats take over,
for,
trampled me into the gutters you did–
now with one gigantic, deformed hand
I pull you there
coitus interruptus
tears that go unnoticed
youth forbidden
Jesus H. Christ
I'm not going to take another beating –
the Devil stirs within me –
hell can be a dark memory

43
Power

do you hear power
the deformed bard
with red, swoollen glans
and dented lyre?
what disease does he carry?
does he have the clap
from cavorting to win favour?
does he have the common cold?
what? no cure?
is power to fall
by the common man's call?
will he die in the carnage
that took innocent lives?
his song
is warbled
by corruption–
devoid
of the chasteness
that simplicity brings.

44
Heritage

a tall gangly akward youth
teeters precariously high on a skyscraper
and systematically jerks off
dispersing
adolescent yearnings
on innocent bystanders teeming below
leaving them to wonder
if it be rain
or
if it be pain
desire mixed with dirt
for it was those before him
who
worked the chaingangs
fought the wars
fucked the women
(and men, prisoners)

it was they
who built concrete jungles
and bootlegged during prohibition
they sodomised their mistresses
and divorced their wives
and this gangly youth is left high and dry
he needs to learn how to screw
to keep the family fortune in the family
but underage
he ain't even no hooker's bait
manhood thrust upon youth
finds him precarious on the edge of a sky rise
engaged in a man to mickey exercise
arise!

45
Massah

The servant hobbles the dry land, head bent

who massah, who the slave?

is dependence not a type of submission?

do they not know the real power?

the soldier, broken, on crutches

mends fences

on

the veld.

a voice cries out

reverbrating in echo over the vast, deserted
expanse:

“massah, tomorrow you make me my morning
tea.

today, today, i clean out the piss.”

46

I and You–True Blue

Do you ever think
of going for a swim
in your birthday suit?
the seahorse would gape
at the splendor
and the shark
would look
twice
the clam would open wide
do you ever think
of walking around
in a crowd
stark naked
without
a stitch on?
boy, do you ever think of me
when you're doing it?

47
Truly Blue

I'm a zero-fidelity girt
scratching, spitting, two-timing
i had a man
whom i couldn't have
and the seconds
turned into minutes,
into hours,
into days,
in the wilderness
and i plunder my soul bare
as i wonder around
in tattered rags
on the outskirts of the citadel
and at the limits of my sanity

48

Yesterday Once More

These are unspoken words
as we disentangle ourselves from the tousled sheets
of our love-making
it is the morrow
and today has come and gone
in the primrose garden
only one petal flowers
as i walk down the well-defined cobbled path
these are the unspoken words
that i nary dare to even whisper
and once more today has come and gone
hear the Shenai playing yearningly
beckoning to wine and lust
tonight duty dictates i felicitate my bethrothed
and when he falls into slumber
will the tears fall
filling a silent void of longing for yesterday

49
Identity

Africa,

land of my birth

beckoning to the prodigal daughter

understanding that some things aren't easy in this life

you hold me sway under your spell

as I try to break the shackles of the present

I, solitary woman,

take the lashings

the loads,

the weight of the chains that bind,

proudly,

with head held high,

as you have taught me—

together we will emerge in victory.

50
Cacophony

My music
is the grating noice
of the broken souls
of a people
devastated by warfare
does anyone really care?
the torn strings of my guitar
splayed apart
like a drunken hussy
my fingers bleed
from trying to mend
and as the woman
coughs and retches
the music disappears

PART-VIII

WORLDS

51
Runaway Girl

You got a life to live

A career to make

You gotta be true to yourself

For your own sake

We only live once this side of life

Climbing the echelons to the skies

The echoes still reverberate of your hurt-filled cries

Still alive and knocking on heaven's gate

Baby, some think you got it made.

Ain't no one bothered to look into your heart

Sometimes they treat you like royalty

Later the same throw you dirt

Anywhere you go you feel locked up

Runaway girl

Running from what life's forced you to be

You can only be free

When other people see

That you ain't no doll to be played with recklessly

You love a man

Against society's will

You rid yourself of life's baggage

But you ain't taken no vow of chastity

Living in your self-made nunnery

You can never be free

Coz at heart

You are a runaway girl

Run, baby, run

An' live life to the fullest

You know it ain't all frolick and fun

Never expecting anything from anyone

The harsh lessons of life have been learnt

All the hopes in your soul have been burnt

You are the runaway girl

You gotta stand tall

On life's catwalk

Because fighting it out

Is what life's all about

You got my best wishes, runaway girl

And maybe, just maybe, sometimes in life's

crazy whirl

You'll find the dreams stored up in your soul

And you'll stop running

Because your dreams themselves will be reality

on the roll.

52
A Closed Door

Rejection
Bondage
Clandestine meetings
of lovers and spies
Loss,
When the wartime hero returned,
Trudges away, beret in hand, fatigues dusty
From the lonely, silent house of his beloved
The only remaining relic to the past:
A closed door.
Servility,
To "accepted" norms
Why can't we make it outside instead of inside?
Domination,
An unequal distribution of power,
By those who closed the door.

53

Is It Really More Beautiful

Is a glittering de Beers diamond
Really more beautiful
Than charcoal?
Both of the same substance
Only in a different form.
Different shape.
The black man, browbeaten in the ghetto
Faces an interminable wait
For death;
As does the
White President,
despite the elaborate security system, deceitful
For none can combat that final foe.
Now tell me.
Is it really more beautiful?

54

The Swan's Last Song

Nero watched Rome burn

Marie advocated:

"Cakes, if not bread"

On the run

Someone stated:

"Venus is the sister of Napoleon."

In the Lake District

Bloodied and mutilated, feathers splotched in red

The swan pitifully trilled its last song

"Ignorance is the hallmark of the human

He cannot face truth

That's why I'm dying

For my words did not soothe

He talks about eco-friendliness

Conserving us

Puts up posters

Organises charity get-togethers

'Preserve the wild life'
he states in grand tones
Yet when we fail to obey
He throws stones
Poaches us
Drapes our furs
Hangs our hides over the fireplace.
I must make haste
For the end is drawing near
And I can no longer sing so clear
Lock them up
Instead of us
In a zoo — specimens of ignorance
Make better spots of amusement,
It's said to be true.

55

Money Making Machines

We see
Directors sitting tight in their seats
Employable individuals with their bowls.
Coppers outstretching their hands on their beats
Mafia underdogs planting bodies in holes.
His day begins hot and sweaty
He ain't got no rush to be ready
No job, no cash
He looks at his last supply of hash
He's got no delivery till evening fall
He waits for the Godsent call
The MD sits in his plush office
Air-conditioning humming smoothly
Things are certainly moving satisfactorily
$400,000 more of skimmed money
He can buy his mistress an apartment
In the fancy highrise
When the Gods so decide, you can touch the skies
The shiksha entertains her last client of the night

This one ain't lettin' go without a fight
He slaps her hard across the face
Then pulls out the money
And leaves at a fast pace
With a child to support, she has to pay the price
Hot-shot son of a political big wig.
Son of a gun
Every one knows where his pop's money comes
from
Money making machines
Give great charity
Only out of expediency
No heart
No soul
While the urchin's shoeless feet
Burn on the melting tar
Of life's street.

56

Dancing By Moonlight

I remember
Dancing
By moonlight
Safe and warm
In your strong, gentle arms
Lured, into believing
You'd keep us
From harm
By our secret little shrine
Near the sea
The swishing of ripples amongst the weeds
And then you left me
And I long for your tender caresses
And I long to hear
The words you now
Whisper
Into the ears
Of another

Caressing her
As you did me
I long for the jangle of the phone
Hoping against hope that you're coming home
Coming home back to me
Now I dance alone
By moonlight
Divided in trance
One part, you, now lost, the other, me
Oh, harsh, harsh, harsh, is reality
I dance lost in thought
Tired of my solo act
And I think of my pact
I wish you love wherever you are
But I...
I still dance alone by moonlight
Every night
Ever since you left
Only half the shrine remains
Down by the sea
And when the weeds rustle
I hear them calling your name
Crying for you to come back
And once again dance
Dance again with me
By moonlight.

57

A Shatfered Mirror

When do we face reality?
In looking at our image
In a shattered mirror
The smiles we once carried,
A grimace
The eyes that once gleamed,
Cracked by worldly knowledge
The features a lover once traced,
A stranger.
Did life do this to us?
Life and living?
Or do we do it to ourselves every time
Looking into reality
Unable to face it's ugliness;
Its truth.

58
The Cross Roads

there's a goodbye in every hello
contact forms separation's edge
the flight of time divides,
you,
the one you love
silence,
harsh awareness
rarer moments foretold
the crossroads
time permits but one final profiled look
what could be
never can
memories till dust
by the suppressed void within
time conquers
again.